Jo-Lynn's Written

Expressions *1*

Jo-Lynn's Written

Expressions *1*

Jo-Lynn Herbert

Purposeful Publishing & Consulting
Email: admin@purposefulpublishing.org
Phone: 530-205-3482

© 2018 by Jo-Lynn Herbert. All rights reserved
Second Revision

No part of this book may be reproduced, stored in a retrieval system, or transmitted by any means without the written permission of the author.

Published by Purposeful Publishing & Consulting
Copy Editor Angela Garcia
Cover and Back Cover Photo by Carlos Clarke (619) 243.4786

ISBN: 978-1947970021

This book is printed on acid-free paper

PRINTED IN USA

Because of the dynamic nature of the Internet, any web addresses or links contained in this book may have changed since publication and may no longer be valid. The views expressed in this work are solely those of the author and do not necessarily reflect the views of the publisher, and publisher hereby disclaims any responsibility for them.

Jo-Lynn's Written Expressions 1

Freedom to write from within to reach you and all
Written by Jo-Lynn Herbert, MSW San Diego, CA

December 15, 2013

2013 has been the most second challenge of my life.
I have learned so much about myself, family, friends and people in this world.
I just returned from my road adventure.
I drove to New Mexico when I felt broken, disappointed and knocked down.
God protected and guided me.
I drove east and didn't look back.
I needed this trip more than I knew.
I visited my sister who lives in New Mexico in an oasis of a beautiful house and nature,
between a mystic mountain and open spiritual ground.
God created such a beautiful majestic earth.
I saw and felt sceneries that are overwhelmingly gorgeous.
The trip was for me to get away and hide,
but God had another plan who allowed me to be,
Emotionally, Spiritually, Mentally,
Filtered & Enlightened.
I have gained new energy and insight without the stress and burdens of heaviness that had taken over me previously for three years.
I began to expect the unexpected to move my goals into reality.
To feel whole is to feel inspired.
To enjoy all the new experiences and opportunities that is within my reach.
I promised that I will always Pray, Praise, Work and be Grateful for my journey of Life, Love and Enlightenment for Advancement!
P.S   I started writing to you and all.

Jo-Lynn Herbert

CONTENTS

1. I Have Something to Say
2. Br=oke
3. Let's Get $ Upgraded
4. Sky View
5. Downgraded
6. In My Midst
7. Triple Strength Return
8. Low Rider
9. To The Avenue
10. No Boundaries
11. Block Rocking
12. Foot Steps
13. Love You Girl!
14. How Easy We Forget
15. Lost Opportunity

16. Unwind from PTSD
17. Music of Life
18. Writing
19. Heart Pain
20. Genuine
21. Denial 2 Truth
22. We Met
23. In the Next
24. Danger Zone
25. Max 'n' Flow
26. Button Down
27. Whisper
28. My Name Is What
29. To My Jaden
30. Be Thy Angels

Acknowledgements

I fully acknowledge, "Special Love & Thank You," To my Ramirez and Herbert Family

To my loving mother Antonia Lopez-Ramirez. To my father the late John Marvin Herbert. To my siblings: Lydia D., John M. Jr., Maynette, Phoenicia and Rami J. My nephews and niece: Marquise S., Tyler J., Shaimir J., Khaydee, Jonathan J., and Selena. Including a heavy host of family and lifelong friends: Wilson P., Geraldine K., Stephanie E., Angelique L., Anita M. and Desean B. to name a few.

My neighbors who became our family: Luz, Juan, Anthony, Angelina, Jennifer, Nadilyn, Juan Jr. and Maritza. To my beautiful daughter, DeAsia Nyomi-Lynn, who asked a significant question at age ten, "can we go back?" (To Church) at a time we were both in sorrow. As an adult who listened to her heart to name my grandson Jeremiah Javier-Anthony. Deep Loving Regards to Love Gospel Assembly, Bronx, NY for the Spirit of Praise that became louder than our deepest sorrow.

"I can't forget true Hip Hop the blast of a fire hydrant and the home of the Caribbean. I acknowledge life comes sometimes in a wonder. When it happens, we try to figure it out, I'm no different. I'm still wondering how these expressions came about.
Never expected all that came from within
Even with a song of praise in my spirit with Peace and Love in my heart while experiencing success, pain and failures, I was reminded yet again, there's no full control of one's own life.
The site of Black Mesa Mountain NM, USA was a surprise as I received an amazing gift.

Dedication

I dedicate my expressions
To a life that led me
To a Spiritual Site
Never to be forgotten
That sparked a dim internal flame

*

In loving memory
To my son
Jaden Maurice Brown
August 29, 1998
On a cold day of
January 10, 1999
Our Heavenly Father called him home

*

Jaden you are deeply missed!
Still feeling you in my arms and heart
Still seeing your sister,
jumping up and down with smiles and
excitement when she first saw you.

JO-LYNN HERBERT

I Have Something to Say 1/11/14jh

*Yeah, I am here
Living
With the truth
I want to talk to you, I want to feel you, touch you, and then be still with you.
I have something to say
I'm from the Bronx.
I will always have something to say and it's up to me
to say what I feel.
I have been here, there, and everywhere without a passport,
then I met you
You!
Who I did not expect
The unexpected is the one to look out for
Why?
because the unexpected always brings more than expected.
I don't want to be on your shit
I don't want you to think you are the shit
Because then our relationship will definitely change for the worse
I would not deal with you
But I will tell you now; I'm feeling more than expected
Why?
Because you are the one I see, feel, and want
The problem is that I don't know if you are ready for me I am not
the one to be played with
I could leave you, play you, and/or ignore you
Which one do you want?
Depends on how you make me feel
So what's up?*

Jo-Lynn's Written Expressions Book 1

Br=oke 1/18/2014jh

I am flat broke!
It's not fun!
This is when you feel life is too short and want some now relief
Relief of reading a book, some sunshine, a downtown trip
To be reborn again
But nothing is better than
A prayer of praise
A touch from someone who touches you the right way
Or the right cold glass of wine or Long Island Iced tea
Or it could be those
Eyes lips & everything in between
That makes you go damn!
I'll save you a trip to the couch or inpatient status
Find a man!
Find a woman!
Find what brings you closer to a lifetime goal
Whichever your preference
Take praise with you
Go find one
Forget being broke
Add an addition to life
Instead of focusing on the minuses of life
Create your own economic twist
Being broke while loving isn't living
It's overreaction
It's surviving
It's dependence
It's bullshit!
So free yourself

JO-LYNN HERBERT

Add praise in your life
create your own economic twist
whichever your preference
go find one
Be free with independence
$ Freedom
Creativity
Accountability
For independent success

Jo-Lynn's Written Expressions Book 1

Let's Get $ Upgraded 1/18/2014jh

*Once I was a licensed life insurance agent able to sell
Insurance
Why?
Because I'm tired of seeing people broke
Imagine this…, I'm broke!
I can imagine it…, why? Because I'm broke
I was a life insurance agent
I've learned a lot
what I've learned in the field is that
along with working as a social worker having had a lot of
face to face time with individuals and families
A lot of problems can be avoided if $ was available.
They say money is not everything or important
Yeah right
Can't pay bills from being broke
Can't have independence from staying broke
I'm tired of seeing people broke
Why people are so broke?
We have to get back to promoting each other
And building each other up
An option that can be done is having Life Insurance
Not leaving your family stranded
We have to understand that death is just as important as
living.
We see death every day but we don't see daily wealth.
Death benefits come in a lot of different ways
If we can talk about welfare benefits we can talk about*

JO-LYNN HERBERT

death benefits
If we can talk about applying for Sec 8 we
can talk about death benefits
While we're getting our pedicure, nails & hair done and at
the car dealerships talking about the latest style of clothes,
shoes or concerts and who got what
we can talk about life insurance
So the best thing to do is to talk about life insurance with
psychotherapy
To figure out why we're broke
To reevaluate how we are surviving
We all need it

Diversity is represented
From all backgrounds and tongues
A paycheck away from being without one
If you are blessed to have a paycheck
So don't get it twisted

Let's get it straight, everyone should have life insurance
Just the same as having medical insurance and a career
Let's get upgraded with medical and life insurance
With progressive positions of having
progressive income
Security would be available for everyone

Jo-Lynn's Written Expressions Book 1

Sky View 1/18/2014jh

Excited!
Turned on
Not knowing
That the unexpected is in my midst
Mentally trying to figure it out
But I can't
Feeling the flow of loving it
Emotionally flagged
Feeling it
The unexpected brings me high to the sky
Sky view of what's coming
Feeling as it is too much to be real
With the right touch of loving and style
Bringing the right mix of physical man
Is it the eyes or the eye stare?
Is it his lips as gorgeous as his eyes?
Is it his grip of intelligence?
That is messing with my sexual peak of want and exploration
He brings it out
Always at the right time of now
At the right speed, shade and depth
The unexpected brings me high to the sky
Sky view of what's coming
At the right mystic of sexiness and roughness
Always at the right time, place & rhythm
Take me yesterday, today and tomorrow
So no beat is undone
Are you able to handle me?
As I'm able to handle you
Of the sky view of what is coming

JO-LYNN HERBERT

Downgraded 1/18/2014jh

Don't move to the left
Don't beg don't brag
    You have been downgraded
    Don't have to worry
    Don't have to figure it out
    I urged you not to take me for granted
    I urged you not to act as if you are all that
    My creativity & expressions of feelings
    Are very sensual and dramatic
    As feelings are true to the soul
    As soul is true to the wind
    From sun down to sun up
    Feelings are alive, proven and valid
    So don't trip
    We are still alive as alive can be
    With awareness & understanding
    I feel more confident, alive & wise
    To the fact I understand how you roll
    As I will stand up & be stronger
    With my feelings in check
    I can breathe you in and out
    Without hesitation or adversity
    So I'm here as you are
    So let's be together
    Learn, grow, forgive & love
    As our willing to love
    Is as important as all else

Jo-Lynn's Written Expressions Book 1

In My Midst 1/18/2014jh

In my midst
There is confusion
Unemployment
Rejection
In my midst
There is creativity
Knowledge and wisdom
Blocked at the highest level of career achieved
Where do you go from here?
Take it to the keyboard and screen
Take it to the masses
And be free
Express heaviness of all inner turmoil
Bust out the truth
Of feelings & insight
Why aren't interview questions respecting
diverse knowledge?
It's who you know, want a best friend?
Looking for the best fit
Go to Social Media
Social media has benefits
Need to eat, need to buy gas and pay rent.
Are you able, willing and ready
to look in the mirror
without expecting the same?
Already have a best friend.
Personal expressions should be screened
how decisions effecting our environment
to include or exclude.
Are you able to look at truth?

JO-LYNN HERBERT

To accept change from within
To make life worth living and acceptable
Diversity should be open and accepted for growth
Look with an open point of view to give the best chance for
All
Cultural competency should be seen
Respect for human beings should be seen
So, in my midst
My mind keeps running
Still living, alive & well
Still creative with knowledge flowing
Making my own way through unrelenting turmoil
But I refuse to stand still in this midst
Of all this turmoil
Need to bust out
Need not to be intimidated
It's time to go, to move forward, bust out, and rise
And allow my creativity to be inspired
To be free
To reach you and all

Jo-Lynn's Written Expressions Book 1

Triple Strength Return 1/11/2014jh

Simply living again
Feeling & Creating
To breathe of something anew
Bringing me to this now
Yesterday was my lift
Tomorrow is my gift
Today is my living
I'm alive
Naturally hidden gifts are arising
To the strength of my gifts
Rising daily
A triple return strength
Of breathing to
feel & create
Bringing me to this now
Yesterday was my lift
Tomorrow is my gift
Today is my living
To live
To breathe
To create from within
To feel my triple return strength
Arising daily

JO-LYNN HERBERT

Low Rider 2013jh

Into my destiny to caress my freedom of mind

To the ecstasy of the understanding of time

Never taking the ever ending high road

But a low rider caress of time

To enjoy the bliss of life

Never missing a beat

But enjoying the caress of time

Freedom of mind is where my soul lays

Caressing the ecstasy of time

Never missing a beat

Walking into my time of beat

Wishing, acknowledging & sharing

As I go by

Never taking the ever ending high road

But a low rider caress of time

Jo-Lynn's Written Expressions Book 1

To the Avenue 2013jh

Where has it all gone?

The avenue street beat

The august sweat beat

The skylight of long lasting

Beats, dreams and articles

Always beaming

To the beat of the Avenue

Stars, rhymes and poems

Mixing like a hot beat

Where has it all gone?

My heart still beats

To the memory of heart pumping

Sweating to the beat

Never again to reenact it

Only to find that my heart carries the beat

Where ever I chose to be

JO-LYNN HERBERT

No boundaries 2013jh

The boundaries of the heart

Where can I take your bliss?

Where can you take my bliss?

Let's pass the line of boundaries

To the moment of long lasting

No cliché here to speak of

But a limitless sense of bliss

How can we share us

Without boundaries

and clichés?

The bliss of us

Without limits of time and space

No boundaries of love

How far can I take your bliss?

How far can you take my bliss?

To share no boundaries of bliss

To share with you and all

Jo-Lynn's Written Expressions Book 1

The living of this world

To know that love affects all the living

Children are our living future

Why wait?

Why be still?

Why not be unselfish?

To allow for them to grow with their bliss

With love, guidance and loving sternness

You and I will be loved more

Having no boundaries to speak of

Only to enjoy the bliss of life

JO-LYNN HERBERT

Block Rocking 2013jh

Rocking to the block
Of the beat
Each block to their own beat
Which mixes to the:
East to the West
West to the East
South to the North
North to the South
How well independence goes with the beat
Independence is not a question
It's a lifestyle
Choice
Of will and heart
Rocking to the block
Of the beat
With mixes of the beat to the:
East to the West
West to the East
South to the North
North to the South

Jo-Lynn's Written Expressions Book 1

Foot Steps 2013jh

Wherever my footsteps lead me

I hope they will be beside you

Wherever my footsteps take me

I hope our footsteps are dancing into the night

Life is full of steps to take

It could be lonely in a world of many crossroads

I wouldn't want to be alone when I know I love you

And we can have each other in a world of many crossroads

So I know our footsteps can withstand any crossroad

Together today our footsteps will walk in love

Dancing into crossroads together wherever my footsteps lead me I hope they will be beside you wherever my footsteps take me I hope our foot steps are in step Together

JO-LYNN HERBERT

Love You Girl! 2013jh

I know I love you girl
Free
Free to be me
Free to say hi to friends passing by
Free to breathe
Relationships Oh My!
Relationships are unpredictable
Love is not
Time is of the essence
To breathe
To live
To smile
Free to be me
Free to say hi to friends passing by
Free to breathe
Relationships oh my!
Relationships are unpredictable
Love is not
As I must say
I know I love you girl
You can predict my love for you
This will never change
Because I love you girl!

Jo-Lynn's Written Expressions Book 1

How Easy We Forget 1/21/2014jh

I love Martin Lawrence

I love me some Martin

    But can you imagine being on a date with Martin

        Yeah, Martin Lawrence, Wow

        Can you imagine?

        Getting cozy with him

Being warm & comfortable

Enjoying eye to eye contact

    Then you start closing your eyes to kiss him

        And you open your eyes slowly

        And then

    (Jump up in a shock) because it's, "Sheneneh!"

        Oh God!

        Some Déjà vu stuff

Then you mentally say it's me, it's not him I guess

I watched the show too many times

    Then you focus reminding yourself it's just a dream

    Then you close your eyes to kiss again

        Trying to get back into the mood

        Then you open your eyes again

    And open them again and it'," Jerome."

        My god and then you jump

    And Martin is saying "what's up with you girl"

JO-LYNN HERBERT

Then you say "you're so hot" And you're so overwhelming feeling good to me "Maybe it's time for me to go home" Then he says being a gentlemen, "ok, I'll take you home" You say "thanks, I enjoyed this time with you" He says, "Likewise."

And at the door he reaches to give you a kiss
And you forget & you close your eyes again
Because it's going to be a quickie kiss
Thinking no big deal
Then you open them and you see,
"MAMA PAYNE."
To you,
Martin Lawrence
Love you

Jo-Lynn's Written Expressions Book 1

Lost Opportunity 1/21/2014jh

*Been through so much
Financially, I lost a lot because of this and that
Money was meant to come and go right?
O.K. for some people is a yea because
They got $
Others say nay because they're broke
I get it
So the less $ I had
I noticed my conversations changed
My conversations turned into finding creative ways to make money
So I mentioned Yeah,
If I don't get any money soon I'm going to have to find a pole
I'm going to have to drop it where it needs to be
bottom of that pole
Not because it's hot but because it's broke
And up like a skyrocket, down like see saw
But it will be worked out on a pole
A pole!
Can you believe an option would be to get on a pole?
But then I thought I need a pole in my bedroom to practice
Then I remembered I have no $ for a pole
Hot damn!
Another job opportunity lost*

JO-LYNN HERBERT

Unwind from PTSD 1/21/2014jh

Past and Present Day Slavery
Unemployment
Street and entertainment violence
Selfishness
Violent TV scenes
Crazy exes and yes
Current boyfriend and girlfriend relationships are included
Racism
Discrimination
Heart breaks
Not being bi lingual
Being asked by an interviewer, 'Do you speak Spanish?'
When they don't speak Spanish either
Sometimes wanting to ask, "Do you?"
Crazy bosses
Crazy aunties
My auntie RIP
My auntie was very funny.
She would call me on my birthday and sing the whole
Happy Birthday song
When I turned 30, I wanted to say get over it!
With a sparkling smile in my heart.
The same loving aunt called the hospital while I was having
early life or death labor
And thought wow, that's nice of her
Then the nurse comes in with hesitation to say
'your aunt said,'
'That's what you get!'
I was like wow, with pain, tears & shock

How funny became a danger zone for me. A new episode of PTSD with everything else began so we all have PTSD & have the ability to bring others to have it

Which are you?
A bully or a healer
A player or a lover
A thief or a giver
We can unwind from PTSD
How, you ask?
True self-reflection
Self-monitoring
Meditation
Knowledge
Forgiveness
And awareness of consequences of hidden and overt Behaviors
That can change a person's day or life Being pro-peace & being pro-healing

JO-LYNN HERBERT

Music of Life 1/22/2014jh

Music came from everywhere
Even in silence
Music was soon to come
Music was calm
Erratic
Bumping
Memorable
You knew music carried a message
All kinds of messages
Even in silence
You became the beat
The beat of the music
Music came from everywhere
The street, the sirens, the waterfall from the fire hydrants, the dancing, the food
Even in sexing
Music became protection
The beat of the heart
The beat of life
Feeling self is to feel music of life
You became the music

Jo-Lynn's Written Expressions Book 1

Even in silence
Music came from everywhere
Even in a tear
Saying goodbye to a loved one
Never in silence
Music was soon to come
Elevator music turned into street music
With an open door to it all
Louder the music the better
Clouded out the noise of chaos and confusion
Into a quiet world of possibilities, peace & joy
Within a city beat to chill & think
Music came from every where
The city became the beat
The beat became the people
The people carried the beat
The beat became the heart
A city girl like me
Is a beat
Never alone because I'm still feeling
The beat of my own beat wherever
I feel it to be

JO-LYNN HERBERT

Writing 1/22/2014jh

First of all writing soothes the soul
And proves that you have a soul
Second of all
It proves you're able to write, learn & convey
As your mind, body, heart & soul becomes one with me
To the public, the masses and most of all to you
The reader, of my environment & the words I hear
Entering something new
Where personalities take form and shape
Writing does the soul good
It brings me together with you
To the public, the masses, and most of all, to you
I may express myself to a person who is not ready
The most powerful spirit of writing
Is the ability to express self, to be understood and to share
Covert and overt expressions of life
Whether you're ready or not
Here I come
With a written word from my mind, body, heart & soul
Hear me, read me
Most of all

Jo-Lynn's Written Expressions Book 1

Accept my writing because it's coming from a place
Of unselfishness
To the public, the masses, and most of all to you
I'm sharing myself with you
From a secret place from a truthful place
Where I stand
To you in spirit & truth
Writing is my speed engine of
All kinds of me
So enjoy me, take me in, and test me.
The joys of writing are alive
To share is to bare all
No shame here!
To the public, the masses, and most of all to you
Writing is to come as one
To express self
To be understood
And to express life
Being worth living
as it was created to be

JO-LYNN HERBERT

Heart Pain 1/24/2014jh

If you are running from my feelings

You are running from me

If you are running from being loved

You are running from life

You are truly a person who has been hurt with deep pain

A pain you have been living with every day

Longer than willing

For you to not want a new feeling

That will allow you to be elated

With the one who loves you

The one you say you love

Capturing intimacy and loveliness

Says in extreme measures

You have been hurt

Not trying to prescript your past, present or future

Not trying to change your mindset

Not trying to push the issue

But I know that I can feel that rock

If I keep hitting it without penetrating the core of you

Then the circle of hurt continues

& eventually this will involve my feelings

In which I already feel the knot

Of the rock

The wall The pain

Where should we go?

        To the left or straight

Should we go in unison or separate

Don't want to play hide & seek

Don't want to delay the loving

Again, where should we go?

JO-LYNN HERBERT

GENUINE 1/19/2014jh

You are a genuine good person.
I am a genuine good person.
I am aware we are both good genuine people indeed
With edges that are intrigued in nature
Maybe or not
That's the reason I am so attracted to you
I am so into you and your gifts it is at times overwhelming.
I haven't written you this kind of inviting note lately
I had something to say
Don't want to sing the same old song
I want to use new strategies
I want to plot & do
Using different words
Different point of view
A new level of being
Using different kinds of money maker routes

Yes, you do
Inspire me
Spark me
Entice me
It's all you
This is new

You
The unexpected!

Jo-Lynn's Written Expressions Book 1

Denial 2 Truth 1/26/2014jh

The hardest thing in life to fight against is love or truth
Or to love somebody who doesn't want it
Or can't handle it
Love is the most courageous thing a person can do
To love someone
To be unselfish
To be open & bare
To fall for someone without expecting it
Why is love the hardest thing to fight against because the denial can go a long way & deep
To actually feel for someone other than yourself
To be in that natural state and not to worry about getting hurt
Or hurting the person you love.
Trust* Devotion* Honesty* Passion* Sincerity* Commitment Sensuality* Care, etc.
are elements of Loving and being in love. You tell me,
I've never been married. So please tell me!
If it's too hard to keep up
In more ways than one
I'm told sooner or later it becomes an assignment, a chore, a job

JO-LYNN HERBERT

So for a single person like me hearing this
It sounds like somewhere down the line in the relationship of love
it becomes confused with a Booty Call
What's date night?
We'll meet up after the game
What's up with that?
If you're telling me love becomes a chore
Or feelings become stalled & confused
It's a booty call
You could be married to your booty call right now!!!
I could hear the ladies saying, "At least I'm married!"
I'm trying to understand if an emotionless relationship is an assignment or a chore
if it feels like a job
It's a Booty Call!!!
Be careful putting a price on it
Forget the important question like
Are we pregnant?
The important question becomes
Is the rent paid?
So you don't need to be in denial anymore
You've just been slammed with the truth

Jo-Lynn's Written Expressions Book 1

We Met 1/29/2014jh

During the late sky
During my dark days
Dying every day
In the midst trying to take a breath
At midway of living
We met
We met
I walked into your eyes
Followed by those lips
How could I resist
Didn't know what to do
We met
We met
During the late sky
During my dark days
Dying every day
In the midst trying to take a breath
At midway of living
We met
We met
I walked into your eyes
Then I walked into your arms
Followed by those lips
How can I resist
Kissing your eyes
Then those lips
Into your caress
I stay
Now my dark sky
Is a spark within an array of brightness?
And my dark days is
A sparkle of breezes of life, laughter and strength
All over me to take in
As I take you in

JO-LYNN HERBERT

In the Next 1/31/2014jh

In the next
I won't doubt
In the next
I won't hesitate
In the next
I won't ask why
In the next
I won't blame
In the next
I won't waste
In the next
I will step forward
I will be wiser
I will be stronger
I will be better
I will still love
Question
Why should I wait for the next or consider
a later or a will?
When I have now
To be wiser
To be stronger
To be better
To move forward
To love and be loved
Later, waiting, will & next
Can never be in me
Because I'm in the now

Jo-Lynn's Written Expressions Book 1

I am confident
Wiser
Stronger
Better
Won't waste my time or yours
Because I am in the knowing of now
Of being confident
Wiser
Stronger
And, Better to love and be loved
Will be in, over, under & kept in your arms wiggling tinkling & kissing you tonight.
1/29/14jh
Being afraid to live is to be afraid of myself.
2/1/14jh
I can't sing, I can't act fake or fake a laugh, but I can write my ass off.
2/3/2014jh
Teach me with an experience not ignorance.
2/4/2014jh

JO-LYNN HERBERT

Danger Zone 2/1/2014jh

We all live in the Danger Zone of life

We fall in love

We have greed

We have suspicion

We talk shit

We test time

We fall short

We all live in the Danger zone of life

We strive to thrive

We keep freedom as thin as can be

We respect to the lowest denominator

We talk shit

We test time

We fall short

We all live in the Danger zone of life

We feel Ghetto life

Jo-Lynn's Written Expressions Book 1

We suffer from drug life

We suffer from discrimination greed

We talk shit

We test time

We fall short

Opposite zone

Creating Setting Motivating Enlightening Redefining Living

Sharing Creating Setting Motivating Enlightening

Redefining Living Sharing Creating Setting Motivating

Enlightening Redefining Living Sharing Creating Setting

Motivating Enlightening Redefining

Living Sharing

Take a risk

Acknowledge

Set yourself free

To honor

To Love

Work successful

Talk in a whisper

JO-LYNN HERBERT

Listen for wisdom

Now in time

Creating Setting Motivating Enlightening Redefining Living

Sharing Creating Setting Motivating Enlightening

Redefining Living Sharing Creating Setting Motivating

Enlightening Redefining Living Sharing Creating Setting

Motivating Enlightening Redefining Living Sharing

Jo-Lynn's Written Expressions Book 1

Max 'n Flow 2/1/2014jh

Dress to the max
Dress to the max
Dress to the max
Dress to the max
Walk in like you know
Walk in like you know
Walk in like you know
Walk in like you know
Max 'n flow
Max 'n flow
Max 'n flow
Max 'n flow
Dance it to the max
Dance it to the max
Dance it to the max
Dance it to the max
Max 'n flow

Max 'n flow
Max 'n flow
Max 'n flow

Take the max to your flow
Take the max to your flow
Take the max to your flow
Max 'n flow

Feel the flow
Feel the flow
Feel the flow
Feel the flow
Max 'n flow
Max 'n flow
Max 'n flow

JO-LYNN HERBERT

Button Down 2/2/2014jh

As I say I love you

I want to do more than say

I love you

I want to button down

& show you my intensity

I want to button down

& give you my time

I want to button down
& share my heat

As I feel you

I want to do more than feel you

I want to button down

& touch you

I want to button down

& feel your thunder

Jo-Lynn's Written Expressions Book

I want to button down
&feel your fire
As I button down

Loving you

Feeling you

I want more of you

Of your thunder

Of your fire

Of you

As I button down slowly

As I button down in front of you

As I button down tonight

I want more of you

Because I want to do more than say

I love you

JO-LYNN HERBERT

Whisper 2/3/14jh

Whisper
Don't scream
Whisper
Don't yell
Whisper
Don't shout
Whisper in my ear
How much you like me
Whisper in my ear
How much you miss me
Whisper in my ear
How much you care
So I could hear your voice
Above the subway noise
Above my busy mind
Above the sirens
Whisper
Don't scream
Whisper
Don't yell
Whisper
Don't shout

Jo-Lynn's Written Expressions Book 1

Whisper in my ear
How much you think of me
Whisper in my ear
How much you're
Feeling me
Whisper in my ear
How much you want to touch me
Whisper

Whisper

Whisper

So I could hear your voice
Above the subway noise
Above my busy mind
Above the sirens
In a whisper
So I could hear your voice
Telling me how much you like me
Miss me & care
In a whisper
I could hear your voice
How much you like me
Telling me how much you think of me
Feeling me
How much you want to touch me
Above the noise
In a whisper

JO-LYNN HERBERT

My Name is What 8/02j

What can I say,
sometimes I don't even know

My name is ...

Upon what condition

Can I say my name

        And be counted

Among you and all

Jo-Lynn's Written Expressions Book 1

To my Jaden from Mommy with Love 2/4/04

In the shining stars

Find my kisses

In the soft clouds beyond

Find my kisses

In the wind of galaxies

Find my kisses

In my heart

Find my kisses

Wherever you are

JO-LYNN HERBERT

Be Thy Angels 2/4/2014jh

Be thy Angels

Come out to strengthen

Be thy Angels

Come out to guide

Be thy Angels

Please forgive

Be thy Angels

Spread love as you go

Be thy Angels

Go find your way

Be thy Angels

Remember us

Remember me

Remember you were loved

Never to be forgotten

Be thy Angels

Be thy rested

www.ingramcontent.com/pod-product-compliance
Lightning Source LLC
Chambersburg PA
CBHW031217090426
42736CB00009B/947